The Secret Everyone Knew Workbook

NATASHA MASON

Created By: Nova Walton Marriott

The Secret That Everyone Knew Workbook

ISBN: 978-1-7354872-4-3

© Copyright 2021 SONSHIP PUBLISHING HOUSE

ALL RIGHTS RESERVED

Reproduction or translation of any part of this work is unlawful. No part of this document may be reproduced or transmitted in any form or by any means, electronic, mechanical, photocopying, recording or otherwise without prior written permission of Sonship Publishing House.

This product us designed to provide authoritative information in regard to the subject matter covered. It is sold with the understanding that the Publisher is not engaged in rendering nor is responsible for legal or accounting services. If legal, accounting or industry specific advice is required, the services of a competent professional in those areas should be sought.

Published by: Sonship Publishing House Inc. www.sonshippublishing.com

Workbook Created by:
Nova Walton Marriott
Hier Self, LLC
www.hierself.com

Cover Design: Vanessa Johnson of Vanessa Johnson Enterprises

CONFIDENTIALITY STATEMENT

This is a comprehensive workbook meant to address various issues arising from child sexual abuse and domestic violence based trauma. It can be for personal use or as a coaching resource. Whatever the purpose, the contents entered shall remain confidential and can only be shared by the contributor of with his/her permission.

Contents

Accountability Statement

To every woman and child that has or is experiencing
some form of abuse, this workbook is for you.

For silent sufferers, it offers an opportunity to speak,
purge and absolve yourself from shame or blame.

Your first courageous step was purchasing this workbook.
That represents your willingness to take the next step in
your healing. It will support you in breaking negative cycles
and achieving self-awareness, closure and acceptance.

As affirmation of change, please sign and date this page and post it
in a visible place as a reminder. Most importantly, take your time.

NAME: ____

Date: ____

CHAPTER 1

Grooming

My mother and I had a complicated relationship. It became even more complicated when she met a new guy, took a liking to him and moved him into our home after a few months of dating him, even after being warned he was abusive.

An alcoholic, before long, he was beating my mother. She fought back so obviously, she knew it was wrong, but she allowed him to stay. I began to frequent family's home more often after that.

It started with him occasionally standing in the doorway of my room. Confused, I didn't say anything at first. Eventually, I blamed myself for failing to tell my mother the first time it happened, thinking I might have nipped it in the bud at that moment.

After the visits to my room continued, I mustered up the strength to tell my mother who told me to tell her if it happened again. The next night, he returned and I screamed out for her. He reacted by walking away but she never came to check on me and didn't mention it the next day either. This hurt me and I didn't tell her when he returned to my room a week later.

This time, he entered my room and sat on my bed. He lifted my nightgown, pulled down my panties and rubbed my vagina.

Frozen with fear, I laid there silent. He said, "You better not tell anybody" and left my room. I quickly pulled the covers over my head and cried myself to sleep but he had set the stage. That was the beginning of his grooming.

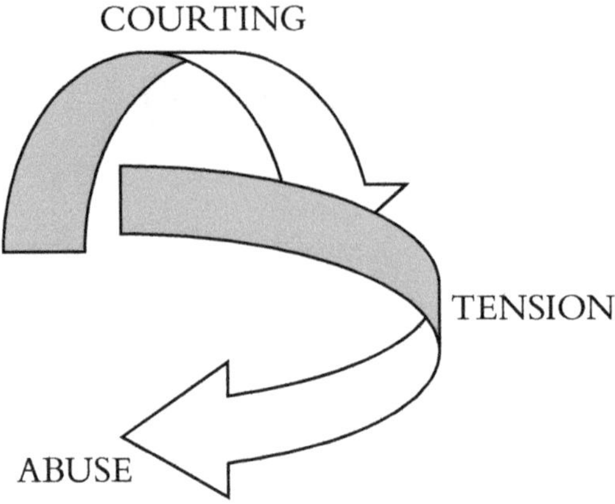

He continued to enter my room and I obeyed his command. I never told; I didn't think my mother would believe me anyway. A few months later, he moved us away from our family and closer to his.

Please explain your line of communication (or lack thereof) with your
parent(s):

____

____

____

____

____

____

____

____

____

Who was your abuser?

____

____

____

____

Please explain in detail how your abuser began grooming you:

Did you tell anyone? Who did you tell? _______________________

If not, what were the inhibiting factors?

____

____

____

____

____

____

____

____

____

____

____

____

____

____

WARNING SIGNS OF GROOMING:

- *Abuser comes on strong in the beginning*
- *Intimidation ("You better not tell")*
- *Charming family and friends of the victim*
- *Isolating the victim from family and friends*
- *Inappropriate physical contact*
- *Encouraging the victim to keep secrets*

WARNING SIGNS OF CHILD SEXUAL ABUSE:

- The child is withdrawn, quiet or angry
- Bedwetting
- The child avoids the abuser
- The child exhibits inappropriate sexual behavior
- Soreness in the genital area
- Fear of being touched
- Forcing sexual acts onto another child

PHYSICAL ACTS OF SEXUAL ABUSE:

- Fondling, touching, kissing private parts; forcing victim to reciprocate
- Penetration with penis
- Inserting fingers, tongue or objects into the vagina or anus

TIPS FOR PARENTS:

- Talk to your child as early as possible about stranger danger, boundaries, inappropriate behavior, intimidation and the importance of coming to YOU or an adult they trust, in the event of abuse or threat of.

- Teach your child the proper names of their intimate body parts so he/she is able to describe where they were touched inappropriately.
- **ALWAYS TAKE YOUR CHILD SERIOUSLY**; Investigate the matter.

TIPS FOR THE VICTIM:

- It is NOT your fault.
- Don't keep the abuse secret, even if the abuser tells you to.
- The touching is still WRONG, even if it tickles or feels good.

ACTIVITY:

Role Play

1. What if an adult stops you outside your school or drives up beside you and says your parent told them to pick you up? What would you do?
2. What if a family member or friend enters your room and makes you feel uncomfortable? (i.e. staring, linger presence etc.) What would you do?
3. What if a family member, friend or stranger touches your private parts? What would you do?
4. What if your coach, teacher or minister tells you they want to spend more time with you, begins touching you inappropriately and tells you to keep it a secret? What would you do?

*(Feel free to create other scenarios as you
build the dialogue with your child)*

"Don't play his game. Play yours"

– Rachel Caine

Time for introspection! Use the blank pages to journal your thoughts or any emotions that have come to the surface after completing the previous activities.

CHAPTER 2

The Secret is Out

Living in the new place wasn't so bad, besides missing my family. My mother found work and my abuser would wait until everyone left to violate me.

The contact remained isolated to him putting his hands in my panties and rubbing my vaginal area but, I was eight years old when he went further.

He rubbed vaseline on my vagina and penetrated me for the first time. I told him it hurt, he told me ok but continued. He left the room after he finished.

I still blame myself for failing to tell my mother or anyone else what was happening to me. Although I was being abused, I often felt sorry for my mother as well as I witnessed my abuser mentally, emotionally and physically abuse her on a regular basis. She enabled him and excused his behavior repeatedly.

"A lot of women, including myself in past relationships sacrifice being mistreated in one way or another to feel the love from a man or show him how much they love him"

— Natasha Mason

One morning while getting ready for school, my mother came into the bathroom and asked me if anyone had been touching me. I remember feeling so relieved and thinking it would finally be over. I told her yes and who it was.

> "When you feel caught in the web of childhood abuse, find words to describe it. Write them. Say them. Express them. In safe places, with safe people."
>
> – Jeanne McElvaney

She assured me she would handle it but, I later heard her telling my abuser's family member about it and saying she was unsure of what to do. That night, he was confronted by the family member, denied the accusation, became violent and left the house.

During the commotion, I began to feel as if I shouldn't have said anything. Immediately thereafter, my mother took me back to my home state but a few weeks later, she began speaking to my abuser again, he came shortly thereafter and they got an apartment together; I remained with a family member.

Eventually, my mother came to get me and we bounced back and forth between my abuser's family home and our home state for a while.

Please describe any feelings of self-blame you have experienced. Why?

____

____

____

____

____

____

____

Do you feel like your parent(s) failed you in any way? Describe any feelings of instability. Please explain

____

____

____

____

____

____

____

Please describe any enabling behaviors you learned during your childhood and time of abuse

____

____

____

____

____

____

____

Please describe any feelings of abandonment during your childhood
and/or time of abuse

____

____

____

____

____

____

____

EMOTIONAL RESPONSES AFTER SEXUAL ABUSE:

- Fear/Embarrassment
- Flashbacks
- Difficulty concentrating
- Guilt or Shame (Self-blame)
- Depression
- Sabotaging future relationships
- Lack of Interest in Sex
- Anxiety

SIGNS OF NARCISSISTIC ABUSE:

- Issues of attachment/Co-Dependency
- Weak boundaries
- People pleasing behavior
- Low Self-Esteem
- Self-Destructive behavior
- Enabling

CHAPTER 3

Toxicity v. Healthy Relationships

I spent as much time in my grandmother's house as I could and connected with my aunt who was a little older and positive. One day, while sitting in the dining room, I heard another aunt tell my grandmother that my mother said she would let her children go hungry just to give my abuser her last; I was beside myself. I didn't want to believe my mother would ever do such a thing. My grandmother insinuated that my mother might be jealous of me. I thought, "Why would she be jealous of me?".

I spent every day praying I wouldn't have to go back to my mother's house to live but, I also didn't want her to think I didn't want to be with her. I just didn't want to be with my abuser. I eventually ended up at her house again but, before long, I returned to my grandmother's house.

Please describe a time you exhibited co-dependent behavior with a
family member, intimate partner or friend:

____

____

____

____

____

Please describe any tendencies to people-please:

____

____

____

____

____

What is your interpretation of a healthy parent/child relationship?

____

____

____

____

____

- They come first
- They use guilt to control you
- They seek/demand your attention
- They compete with you (jealousy)
- They make you feel indebted or responsible for them and their happiness
- The child suffers from toxic shame
- Emotionally unavailable

ACTIVITY:

Name some people in your life that make or have made you feel good about yourself:

____

____

____

____

____

____

____

____

____

____

List some things these people have done to encourage you:

____

____

____

____

____

____

____

____

____

____

____

____

"Surround yourself with people who make you happy. People who make you laugh, who help you when you're in need. People who genuinely care. They are the ones worth keeping in your life. Everyone else is just passing through"

— Karl Marx

Violated in More Ways Than One

was back with my mother now because she insisted that I be. It wasn't long before my abuser started coming into my room again. It happened once or twice a week or when he was inebriated. I would lay there crying and he would yell, "Shut up and stop crying!" He would buy me gifts on special occasions, I guess that was his way of "making up for it". He even made sexual advances toward my aunt once but, she hit him with her shoe, ran home, called the police and had him arrested.

He also continued to beat my mother, sometimes to the point of hospitalization. She pressed charges once but still allowed him back into the home. She even stood by his side when he appeared for the charges related to my aunt and asked her to drop the charges; she obliged.

Settled back in at my mother's house, I became friends with a girl in my building. One day, while visiting her house, she asked if she could do something to me. Naively, I said yes and she told me to lay down and close my eyes. She put her hand in my pants. I asked her what she was doing, told her I had to go and left. I never told anyone. After that, she stopped speaking to me.

I spent as much time at my grandmother's house as I could and assisted her at church often as she was a pastor. I found that the worse the abuse became, the more I developed a relationship with GOD. When I was home, I isolated.

How many times (if any) have you been re-victimized? Were the abusers different each time? Please explain

____

____

____

____

____

____

____

____

Please describe any Domestic Violence based incidents you have witnessed in your home and/or experienced directly:

____

____

____

____

____

____

____

____

____

____

____

FACTS ABOUT DOMESTIC VIOLENCE:

- Often takes place in private
- Abusers blame the victim
- Verbal abuse usually escalates to violence
- The abuser has a need to be in control
- **"Two-thirds of Domestic Violence perpetrators are under the influence of alcohol; One-third under the influence of drugs"—Darlene Lancer, JD, LMFT**
- Some abusers suffer from mental health conditions

Plan for safety in the event of Domestic Violence

- Keep a journal of abuse (Dates, threats, stalking, destruction of property). Store it in a safe place
- Keep a packed bag with basic necessities (money, clothing, identification, toiletries etc)
- Ask a trusted neighbor to call 911 if they hear any unusual activity
- Change passwords on all accounts; open a new bank account if applicable and have all information sent to a secure location
- Determine a safe place you can go in the event you have to vacate quickly (Do not leave a paper trail)

Please create your private plan in the area below:

____

____

____

____

____

____

____

____

____

____

____

____

____

____

____

____

____

____

____

____

____

____

____

____

____

____

____

____

"The guarantee of safety in a battering relationship can never be based upon a promise from the perpetrator, no matter how heartfelt. Rather, it must be based upon the self-protective capability of the victim. Until the victim has developed a detailed and realistic contingency plan and has demonstrated her ability to carry it out, she remains in danger of repeated abuse"

— Judith Lewis Herman

CHAPTER 5

Avoidance and Rebellion

We moved again. I would occasionally ride my bike to my old neighborhood until I began to make "friends" in my new one. By then, my mother had given birth to my sister. She doted on her in ways she had never doted on me and that hurt me.

The sexual abuse continued and had become more frequent. My abuser created a regimen that consisted of keeping me home from school on Fridays so he could have sex with me. Again, he told me, "You better not say anything to your mother" and I didn't but, I know she knew what he was doing. He even began to issue idle threats to intimidate me such as, "You know I can stop you from breathing".

The Friday ritual went on until my mother was called to my school about my absences. When questioned, I told her I was home but, my abuser denied my claim and she believed him. I didn't push the issue. To add insult to injury, he was abusing me and sleeping with numerous women in the neighborhood. My mother knew and never did anything about any of it.

Bystander Effect," the surprising fact that many people will stand by while terrible things happen, suggests that when something horrible occurs, people often go into a kind of denial, thinking that if it were really this bad, somebody else would be stopping it

– Peter Ditto

I was only 11 years old, hanging out with neighborhood kids who my mother warned me were not truly my friends and I started developing an interest in boys, specifically, the son of a local store owner. We flirted and kissed a few times and I did whatever I thought would make him happy. Before long, I had sex with him in a hallway. He was my first sexual experience outside of my abuser. After I gave him what he wanted, he started avoiding me. I moved on with life like none of it ever happened. I was used to doing that.

> *"Long-term consequences of sexual abuse may include chronic self-perception of helplessness, hopelessness, depression, impaired trust, self-blame, self-destructive behavior and low self-esteem"*
>
> *— Prevent Child Abuse*

I also became a bit rebellious and failed to follow my mother's instructions a few times. One time, after directly defying my mother, she went home and told my abuser. She whipped me with a rope and he came into my room in the middle of the night, questioned me about my whereabouts, began slapping me and choked me with a rope almost to the point of passing out. That was the first time he physically abused me.

A few months later, I got my menstrual period for the first time and shortly thereafter, at the age of 12, I was pregnant by my abuser and decided to have an abortion aside from my mother's encouragement to keep the child. She later alluded to being against abortions even if the pregnancy was the result of rape or molestation. **She knew what was happening to me** but, I still loved her dearly, was concerned with her happiness and well-being and would do anything to protect or comfort her in her time of need.

Did you understand the abuse was wrong from the beginning? What was going through your mind when it was happening?

____

____

____

____

____

____

____

How did you cope with the trauma of being sexually abused? Was there any acting out or rebellion? Did you seek any intervention?

____

____

____

____

____

____

____

What happened when it was discovered that you were sexually abused (if applicable)? Who was the first to find out?

____

____

____

____

____

____

____

Was your abuser ever brought up on charges? Please explain

____

____

____

____

____

____

____

____

As a victim of sexual abuse, what is your outlook on sexual intercourse, relationships and intimacy? Have you had any bouts with promiscuity? Please Explain

____

____

____

____

____

____

____

____

HAVING STRONG, NURTURING RELATIONSHIPS WITH YOUR CHILDREN:

- Seek help to resolve trauma within yourself
- Be mindful of who you allow to be alone with or in the presence of your child
- Ensure you are meeting your emotional needs through adult relationships, not through your child
- Teach your child about his/her body and how to protect it
- Listen to your child, take interest in his/her life, spend quality time together and keep an open line of communication
- Refrain from physical punishment or humiliation as the first resort

CHAPTER 6

Enabling

My mother was in jail due to her boyfriend's transgressions and my sister and I were living with our aunt until her release. I was 13, hung out with my cousin daily and my interest in boys continued.

My mother was ultimately released and I was happy to have her home. We moved into my grandmother's house and it wasn't long before she started visiting my abuser in prison; she even made me go.

Staying at my grandmother's house was the safest and most stable I have ever felt but, when my abuser got released, we moved into a hotel with him because my grandmother wouldn't allow him to stay in her home. He was home but his behavior didn't change. Drunk one night at the hotel, he beat me with a wire until he drew blood and raped me with my mother laying in the next bed. She pretended to be sleep and he tried to convince me that I had caused him to do it.

> *"I don't know why my mother didn't leave him or why she let the abuse continue with me. I never asked, but maybe I should have"*
>
> — *Natasha Mason*

The sexual and physical abuse continued for any reason he could think of. I've had black eyes, swollen jaws and busted lips causing me to miss days of school but, my mother gave officials sufficient explanation for my absence. That hindered any cause for concern and I wasn't very verbal about my situation so, they had no idea what I was going through.

> *"Child abuse is when a 'caregiver' either fails to provide appropriate care (neglect), purposefully inflicts harm or harms a child while disciplining him/her"*
>
> *– Roxanne Dryden-Edwards*

TYPES OF CHILD ABUSE:

- <u>Neglect</u>-*Failing to provide adequate care, food, shelter, clothing etc.*
- <u>Physical</u>-*Injuries, bruises, scratches, broken bones*
- <u>Emotional</u>-*Damaging a child's self-esteem*
- <u>Sexual</u>-*Innappropriate physical contact*

SELF-THINK:

How do you personally differentiate denial from betrayal?

____

____

____

____

____

____

____

____

How Do I Help My Sexually and Physically Abused Friend or Family Member?

Your friend/family member comes to visit. You're having a great time with him/her when they suddenly become serious. He/she confides in you that they are being beaten and sexually abused by the step-parent and it has been happening for quite some time. He/she begins to cry, says they feel hopeless and don't know what to do. He/she also asks you not to say anything.

- Should you keep it to yourself? Why or Why Not?
- How can you be helpful without betraying his/her trust?

CHAPTER 7

Teen Pregnancy As A Result of Rape

As my abuser had the propensity to commit crimes, he and my mother decided to relocate the family to California when he got wind that there were warrants out for his arrest. I was 14 years old and all I could think about was the family and friends I was leaving behind. I adjusted my outlook when we arrived in California and decided not to form any attachments by way of friendships.

My mother, siblings and I stayed in a shelter and he stayed in the car. We eventually moved to a hotel until we could find housing. One day, feeling sick, my mother took me to the emergency room where I found out I was pregnant for the second time…by my abuser.

My mother didn't say much but, he wanted me to have the baby! I pushed for an abortion but every time my mother made an appointment, he made an excuse to hinder her from taking me. Besides my mother, none of my family knew I was pregnant until my aunt came to visit. She asked me if he was the father and I denied it; I was ashamed to tell her and I didn't want my mother being judged by the family either.

E. Pence & M. Paymar

Eventually, I gave birth to a son and decided regardless of the circumstances and what I had been through, this was my baby and I was going to pour all my love into him.

How were you able to separate the traumatic experience of rape/child sexual abuse from your ability to love a child that was a product of the act? (If applicable)

____

____

____

____

____

____

____

Did you encounter obstacles with bonding along the way? Please explain

____

____

____

____

____

____

____

CHAPTER 8

Looking for Love in All the Wrong Places

Living in Massachusetts and traveling with my mother to Connecticut to see my abuser in jail on the weekends, we were staying in a hotel when I decided to call an old friend. After catching up, we made plans for him to come visit. I cleared it with my mother and he came over that afternoon.

My mother left to visit him and it wasn't long before my friend was asking me to go into the bathroom with him. We had sex, talked a bit afterwards and he left. My mother wasn't concerned about leaving her 15 year old daughter alone with a boy but, she did inquire about where I met him because "he was cute". I asked him to come around because I liked that he gave me attention and affection that I didn't receive from anyone else.

"The abuse I suffered had been so normalized that I stuffed it away. In fact, my abuse had incorrectly convinced me that I had to be sexually desirable to have any self-worth"

— Tia Hollowood

Not long thereafter, we moved back to Connecticut and back into my grandmother's house. I was so glad to be home and around my friends but some of the parents didn't want their kids around me because I was young with a baby. I started attending a local high school and was looking forward to connecting with my male friend but soon found out I wasn't the only girl in his life. I eventually moved on to another neighborhood boy.

He wasn't the most attractive but for some reason, I was drawn to him. We talked off and on for about a year but I wasn't the only girl in his life either. A couple of months later, my cousin introduced me to someone else. I became close with him and we embarked on a relationship that basically consisted of sex and talking on the phone because he never took me out on dates. Eventually, we cooled down but, remained friends.

My abuser was nearing release, started coming home on weekend passes and we would stay at a hotel with him. It felt good to have a break from him for a while; to not have to walk around on pins and needles, looking over my shoulder. I was still talking to my friend on the phone when I could but that was cut short one day when my abuser caught me talking to him on a payphone.

He yelled at me, took me back to the hotel, asked me who I was speaking to and started slapping me. My mother sat there with a bewildered look on her face as if she was asking me why I had done what I had done. I left the physical altercation with a bruise on my face and didn't go anywhere until it was gone. When we returned to my grandmother's house, nobody asked where I got the bruises from.

Feeling sick one day, I suspected I might be pregnant. I took a test and it was confirmed. This time, it was by the guy I had been seeing but, I was afraid to tell him because I knew he would be leaving for college soon and didn't think he would stay in contact with me. Instead, I decided to have sex with the guy I was talking to before him and pass the baby off as his. He was a good person and although I wasn't in love with him, I had love for him. I notified him but it was a while before I got a response.

I moved on with life and eventually reconnected with a guy I dealt with years before. I began sending him gifts and money to pay his phone bill. By then, I had three children and we were talking about having a child together. Eventually, I found out he was talking to someone else but I continued to send him money anyway whenever he asked. I still had hope that we would be together.

I have also talked to guys on chat lines and eventually met someone I chose to move in with because he offered, only to find out he didn't have a job. Once again, I was looking for love and affection and when that didn't happen, I left the relationship looking for someone else instead of working on me and finding everything I needed within myself.

Thinking about it now, I wish I'd had a father figure in my life to teach or show me how a real man should treat me. My biological father was addicted to drugs all of my childhood. I only have a few good memories of him. He is no longer living.

Discuss a time you sought attention from the opposite sex. What was your motivation? Please explain

____

____

____

____

____

____

____

____

- Survivors equate it to self-worth
- It provides an escape from the trauma
- Only way the survivor knows how to relate to others
- Gives the survivor some semblance of control over their body

SELF-WORTH ACTIVITY:

Date:	
My BEST attribute is:	
3 interesting things about me:	
I feel most proud of myself because:	

Going with the Flow

My mother and abuser were talking about returning to California and I didn't want to go. I decided to tell my grandmother what my abuser had been doing to me. She reported it, they questioned me, I confirmed and he was sent back to prison. I was so glad someone finally did something. I wanted the abuse to end (for me and my mother) and my grandmother was the only support I had.

Soon, my mother was telling me I needed to drop the charges and threatening to give my phone book to my abuser's attorney. She said, "I was no angel and she would show the attorney I had a phone book full of boy's numbers". I felt like my back was against the wall because I didn't want anyone to know my business.

Even though it was a regular thing, I was hurt that she took his side over mine. A few days later, I tried to commit suicide by taking a handful of my grandmother's prescription medicine and went to sleep. It was unsuccessful and I woke up a few hours later. I obeyed my mother, called the detective and told him it wasn't true. They closed the case and my abuser was released and sent back to a halfway house.

It wasn't long before he was partying and using drugs. When the authorities got wind, he left the halfway house and showed up at my school with my mother, sisters and son in tow. I was told we were moving back to Massachusetts but, while on the road, he told me we were headed back to California. I kept thinking I'd lost my chance to be happy. I got over it eventually.

I was 16 years old, my mother and abuser knew I was pregnant again and didn't say anything about it. After I had my daughter, he said, "I thought she was mine until you had her because the dates didn't add up". That didn't stop him though. The sexual abuse eventually started again. I also noticed that he didn't hit me when I was pregnant. I looked at it as a temporary break from the violence.

"Adolescent girls in physically abusive relationships were three times more likely to become pregnant than non-abused girls"

— TA Roberts

We eventually moved out of the motel and found stable housing but the physical abuse became worse and more frequent. I tried to convince myself I would take my children and leave when I turned 18 but my abuser had a mental hold on me that prevented that.

One day, he called me into the living room and began telling me how "disappointed he was that I had a baby by someone else; that she should have been his". He was in complete denial about what he had done to me pretty much my entire life. He went on to intimidate me by saying, "Sometimes, I feel like tying up your feet and hands and putting you in a tub of water" or "You know, I thought about shooting you up with heroin but, I didn't want to give you too much and you overdose". I was shaking and asking God not to let him kill me. He eventually had sex with me and I went back to bed.

He created a rule that when he turned the living room television off, I was to come to him so he could have sex with me. If I failed to comply, I would wake up to him beating me; he even pointed a gun in my face once. I conditioned myself to stay up at night and it wasn't long before I was pregnant with my third child. I decided to keep the baby because I knew he wouldn't hit me while I was pregnant.

Eventually, he was taken back into custody and for the first time, both me and my mother were happy about it but he was released shortly thereafter and things went back to normal.

I held on to every "good" moment I could, to include smoking marijuana with them because those times represented peace and quiet. I could also feel my mother's resentment toward me every time there was a "light" moment between me and my abuser. She didn't realize I was doing anything I could to keep him from beating me.

The abuse my mother and I were suffering became a topic of conversation between us. We would take the children to the park and talk about returning to Connecticut or what my abuser had done the night before but, we never discussed what he had been doing to me for years. Eventually, what started as recreational drug use became my mother's crack addiction. This led to shoplifting and a few arrests.

TACTICS NARCISSISTS USE TO CONTROL:

- Rage
- Staring or Threatening
- Projecting
- Manipulation
- Playing the Victim

"People who have survived trauma and abuse often turn to chemical substances to suppress their emotional pain and anxiety"

— Laura Close

CHAPTER 10

Confusion and Clarity

With my mother's drug problem progressively getting worse, my abuser was beating her one night and my sister called the police. They arrested him and she again alluded to me enjoying his advances. That broke the ice! I told her I never wanted him touching me and I just did things to keep him from hitting me. She told me he told her I wanted to have sex and she believed him. Why would my mother believe that? How could she think I wanted him at the age of five? I didn't know what sex was! Did she think because I was older now, I wanted him? I cried every time he touched me. I was afraid of him and she failed to protect me!

I contacted my cousin to see if she could help me buy tickets for me and my children to return to Connecticut. She agreed and told me to let her know how much and when. When the time came near, she stopped answering her phone and before long, a year had passed as I tried to accumulate the money for our tickets myself.

Eventually, I used the ticket I had already bought for myself and returned to Connecticut without my children. Immediately, I felt nothing but guilt. Why didn't I just take my children with me? I could have walked away and never looked back. Honestly, I knew I was going back. I still felt responsible for my mother and was waiting for her to come with me. I was the only one there for her in her addiction.

- Low Self-Esteem
- People pleasing
- Lack of Boundaries
- Caretaking
- A need to be liked

While back in Connecticut, I met a new guy. Things moved really quickly between us and before long, he was asking me to move in but, I told him I had to go get my children. But, hearing someone say it was going to be okay and they cared felt good.

After a while, my aunt paid for my ticket to return to California. I wasn't looking forward to seeing my abuser but, I wanted to see my children and siblings. I knew once I returned, he would make it hard for me to leave again. I had lost a lot of weight and once I got there, wasn't feeling well. I went to the emergency room and the doctor told me I was anemic and PREGNANT again…by my abuser. I kept the baby and began to find solace by attending church regularly with my children. I learned how to create peace for myself by using my time differently, fasting, meditation and prayer.

My mother stopped using for a bit but eventually relapsed and this time, it was out of control. She would leave for days at a time and steal from me but I never turned my back on her. I kept myself immersed in church, despite the abuse I was still experiencing. He even tried to hinder me from being so involved in church and slapped me and choked me once while accusing me of doing more at church than I did at home. This sent me spiraling into depression and I tried to take my life for a second time by taking a handful of pills and going to sleep. By the Grace of God, I woke up the next day. I used to pray to God that my abuser would die because I wanted the abuse to stop. By then, he was hitting me more than he was hitting my mother.

Eventually, he asked me to marry him! He mistook me occasionally looking at wedding magazines as me wanting to marry him. I yearned to be in a real relationship but it was impossible at that time with all I had going on in my household.

A few months later, I found out I was pregnant with my fifth child, again, my abuser was the father. This time, he asked me what I was going to do and I told him I was keeping it. After I gave birth to my daughter, I requested my tubes be tied but, after the hospital tried to gain clearance from my insurance, I was released without the procedure being done and the abuse continued.

One day, after revelation from God, I gathered the courage to take my children and leave. My oldest daughter even agreed to return her cheerleading uniform to contribute to our exit. I talked with my siblings for a few moments, called a cab, took my five children and two huge suitcases and left. I prepared for my departure by calling a domestic violence shelter before I left but, they wouldn't take me because I didn't have any bruises. They gave me an address for another shelter and I caught a cab to the location but discovered they were closed until November.

I had $5.00 to my name to pay for the cab and he was not only gracious enough to tell me to keep my money, he also bought the children something to eat and paid for one night at a hotel for us. He told me he would ask around about a shelter and come back in the morning to let me know. Look at God!

The cab driver kept his word and returned the next morning. He bought more food for the children, said he hadn't located a shelter yet, paid for another night at the hotel and took me to the county office to have my public assistance benefits transferred over. The cab driver picked us up from the office and told us he found a shelter! We got there in time and was accepted. We hit some other snags in the road after that but eventually connected with a church who assisted us in buying bus tickets to return to Connecticut and gave us transportation to the station and traveling money. I was so grateful.

We weren't in Connecticut long before my abuser started calling saying he wanted the kids. Young and naïve, I gave them a choice whether to stay with me or go and three of them chose to go. My oldest daughter chose to stay with me. My youngest was still an infant but, eventually, he came to get her too. Allowing my children to go back to him is my largest regret. I figured if I gave him what he wanted, he would stop contacting me. Eventually, he served me with a restraining order and custody papers.

A guy I was dating advised me to seek assistance through the sexual assault hotline. They agreed to help and asked me for a notarized letter attesting to everything I experienced at the hands of my abuser. I sent everything to the court but, I soon received a letter requiring me to appear. I didn't have the money to appear so, the date came and went. Eventually, I received a letter stating I was allowed visitation but was required to pay $900 per month child support.

HEALING FROM ABUSE AND TRAUMA:

- Forgive but, don't forget
- Be Introspective. Work toward self-awareness
- Seek support and recovery resources
- Release. Tell Your Story

Describe a traumatic experience that caused you difficulty in finding forgiveness. How did you eventually find it?

____

____

____

____

____

____

How has finding forgiveness been vital to your life?

____

____

____

____

____

____

____

Conclusion

As I reflect on my life, I ask myself the same questions over and over again:

1. What if I had told my grandmother sooner? Would that have changed my circumstances?
2. What if I had researched domestic violence more to find out about shelters?
3. Why didn't family reach out to me to help since everyone knew what was happening to me?

I realize although my family and friends knew what I was going through and did nothing, it is pointless to address the "what-ifs" and I must forgive and move forward for my own healing and well-being. My time and energy is better put to use by advocating for victims/survivors of domestic violence and child sexual abuse and telling my story through this book.

I justify my mother's failure to intervene by the fact that she was mentally and physically abused as well. I believe her denial helped her to face another day. He cheated on her repeatedly and brought other women into our home. He disrespected her over and over again, in front of her children. I have since forgiven her and have a close relationship with her. She has finally broken free, lives with a roommate and goes to church regularly.

I have also forgiven my abuser but, there is minimal contact in the present. I had to forgive him completely so all the anger, hatred and hurt I had toward him could dissipate. I decided to give it all to God. I even called him and prayed with and for him. Please understand, I don't trust him and although we are both different people now, I will never put myself in a position to be alone with him. He has never asked me to forgive him, it was a conscious decision on my part. Praying for him helped me break free.

All of my children remain with their father except two. I pray my relationship with my other three children will improve in time. I'm currently married, have another son, live in New York and work for a domestic violence organization helping women like me every day.

Journal...

Use the following pages to journal freely about any thoughts, progress or new perspectives.

____

____

____

____

____

____

____

____

____

____

____

____

____

____

Resources

National Domestic Violence Hotline-800-799-7233

Stopitnow.org

Crisistextline.org

Rainn.org-800-656-HOPE

National Suicide Prevention Lifeline-800-273-8255

References

www.catalystdvservices.org
priority research services, Inc.
www.loyola.edu
www.psychologytoday.com
www.healthyway.com
everydayfeminism.com
www.betterhelp.com
www.businessinsider.com
www. verywellmind.com
preventchildabuse.org
www.medicinenet.com
recapp.etr.org
www.cdc.gov
www.jognn.org
www.healthyplace.com
www.positivepsychology.com
pro.psychcentral.com
www.sunrisehouse.com

Printed by Libri Plureos GmbH in Hamburg,
Germany